hvya

The 1900s

Stephen Feinstein

The 1900s

Stephen Feinstein

Enslow Publishing
101 W. 23rd Street
Suite 240
New York, NY 10011
USA
enslow.com

THEODORE ROOSEVELT
26th President 1901-1909

Published in 2016 by Enslow Publishing, LLC.
101 W. 23rd Street, Suite 240, New York, NY 10011

Library of Congress Cataloging-in-Publication Data

Feinstein, Stephen.
The 1900s / Stephen Feinstein.
    pages cm. — (Decades of the 20th and 21st centuries)
Includes bibliographical references and index.
Summary: "Discusses the decade 1900-1909 in the United States in terms of culture, art, science, and poli-
tics"—Provided by publisher.
Audience: Grade 9 to 12.
ISBN 978-0-7660-6920-6
1. United States—Civilization—1865-1918—Juvenile literature. 2. United States—Politics and govern-
ment—1901-1909—Juvenile literature. 3. Nineteen hundreds (Decade)—Juvenile literature. I. Title.
E169.1.F3529 2015
973.8—dc23

                                2015010942

Printed in the United States of America

To Our Readers: We have done our best to make sure all Web sites in this book were active and appropriate
when we went to press. However, the author and the publisher have no control over and assume no liability
for the material available on those Web sites or on any Web sites they may link to. Any comments or sugges-
tions can be sent by e-mail to customerservice@enslow.com.

Photo Credits: Archive Photos/Getty Images, pp. 21, 36; Art Media/Print Collector/Getty Images, pp. 61,
62, 87 (top); Buyenlarge/Getty Images, p. 45; DEA/A. DAGLI ORTI/De Agostini/Getty Images, p. 53; DEA
PICTURE LIBRARY/De Agostini Picture Library/Getty Images, p. 88 (bottom); DEA Picture Library/Getty
images, p. 52; Edwin Levick/Getty Images, p. 59; Everett Historical/Shutterstock.com, pp. 11, 13, 42 (bottom); Express/Hulton Archive/Getty Images, p. 28; Fine Art Images/Heritage Images/Getty Images, p. 64;
Fotosearch/Getty Images, p. 16; GAB Archive/Redferns/Getty Images, p. 39; Hulton Archive/Archive Photos/
Getty Images, pp. 17, 18, 30, 72, 86 (bottom); Hulton Archive/Getty Images, pp. 31, 88 (top); itsmejust/Shut-
terstock.com, p. 70; Juan Gris/Getty Images, p. 41; Keystone-France/Gamma-Keystone via Getty Images, p.
18; Library of Congress Prints and Photographs Division, pp. 3 (bottom right), 6; MPI/Getty Images, p 69;
Museum of the City of New York/Byron Co. Collection/Getty Images, p. 56; Oxford Science Archive/Print
Collector/Getty Images, p. 23; Phil Schermeister/National Geographic/Getty Images, p. 66; Photo File/Getty
Images, p. 47; Photoquest/Archive Photos/Getty Images, p. 14; Picture Post/Moviepix/Getty Images, p. 33;
PM Images/The Image Bank/Getty Images, p. 34; Popperfoto/Getty Images, pp. 48, 49; The Print Collector/
Print Collector/Getty Images, pp. 3 (top left), 25, 60; Science & Society Picture Library/Getty Images, p. 75;
Science Source/Getty Images, pp. 3 (top right), 76, 79, 87 (bottom); Stock Montage/Archive Photos/Getty
Images, p. 54, 85 (top); Time Life Pictures/Library Of Congress/The LIFE Picture Collection/Getty Images, p.
26; Time Life Pictures/Mansell/The LIFE Picture Collection/Getty Images, pp. 10, 82; Topical Press Agency/
Getty Images, p. 44; Underwood Archives/Getty Images, p. 37; Universal History Archive/UIG via Getty Im-
ages, p. 32; William Thomas Cain/Newsmakers/Getty Images, pp. 3 (bottom left), 22, 86 (top).

Cover Credits: Library of Congress Prints and Photographs Division (Wilbur and Orville Wright); The Print
Collector/Print Collector/Getty Images (Princess Louise); Science Source/Getty Images (Albert Einstein);
William Thomas Cain/Newsmakers/Getty Images (Teddy Roosevelt).

Contents

Introduction 7

Pop Culture, Lifestyles, and Fashion 9

Entertainment and the Arts 29

Sports 43

National and International Politics 51

Advances in Science, Technology,
and Medicine 71

Conclusion 81

Timeline 85

Glossary 89

Further Reading 91

Index 93

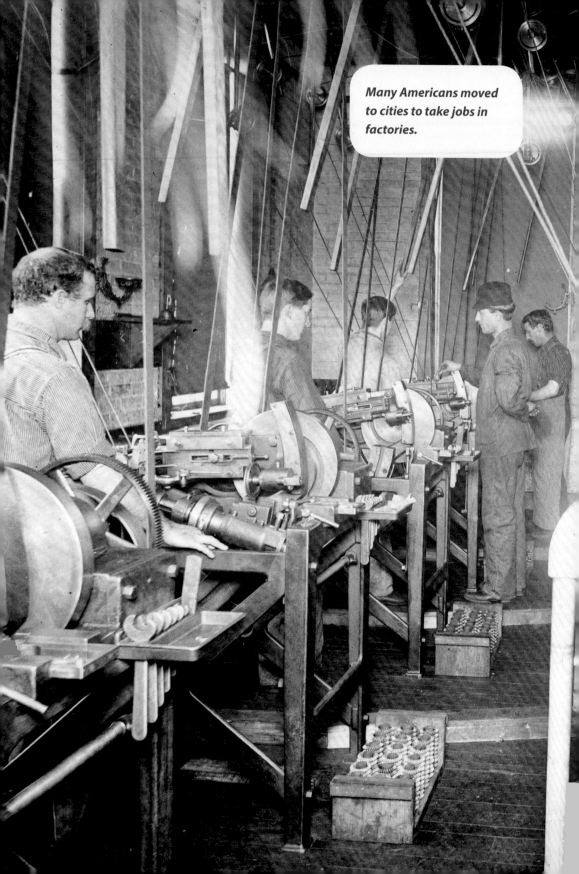

Many Americans moved to cities to take jobs in factories.

Introduction

The year 1900 marked a new beginning. During the nineteenth century, America had grown from a small group of states on the East Coast to a mighty nation spanning the continent from ocean to ocean. The nation had survived a terrible civil war and emerged stronger and better. Countless pioneers made the often dangerous overland trek to the West in covered wagons. America's reputation as a land of opportunity continued to grow at the turn of the twentieth century. Millions of people from around the world who were filled with hopes and dreams for a better life packed their bags and headed to America.

Americans looked to the future with confidence. It seemed that the United States was about to join the ranks of other great powers, such as Great Britain and France. The US Army and Navy became stronger. Americans began taking a greater interest in world affairs. The nation was about to take its place as a major player on the world stage.

In 1900, about 60 percent of Americans still lived in rural areas, mainly on farms. To get to town, they had to hitch up a horse to a buggy. Soon, many Americans would toss away their buggy whips and drive around in their new horseless carriages—cars. Few would have believed that within just a few years, people would travel through the air in flying machines. Work was different, too. People moved from rural farms to cities and took factory jobs. They earned steady wages and bought new products.

Theodore Roosevelt was president of the United States for almost all of the twentieth century's first decade. He was confident and charming. Americans liked his attitude. Roosevelt used common sense to solve problems. He seemed ready for any challenge. The young president helped settle disputes with other countries. He also cracked down on greedy factory owners. Theodore Roosevelt was a bold leader for a bold time in America.

Not all was perfect, however. Many factory jobs were unsafe and paid little. Many families were poor. Children had to quit school to work. They toiled long hours just to help their families buy food. Women were not considered equal to men. They did not have the right to vote. African Americans were often treated poorly, especially in the South. They were denied the same rights as white citizens. It would take years for these inequalities to change.

These problems aside, the first decade of the twentieth century was a time of great excitement and anticipation. The world seemed to be getting smaller. People could send messages quickly over long distances—even across oceans. New machines were being created that would make it easier to travel to faraway places. For fun, people could watch stage plays and sporting events. But film was also getting started. Art, books, and music were also changing as authors and artists began to explore new styles and ideas. The decade 1900–1909 was a time when people looked to the future.

Pop Culture, Lifestyles, and Fashion

The first decade of the new century was exciting. Thanks to the Industrial Revolution, people now used machines to manufacture things and worked together in factories. New inventions were inspired and followed by gains in science and medicine. People began living longer.

The Expansion of Urban Areas

A massive wave of immigration began around 1890. This continued during the first decade of the 1900s. Almost nine million men, women, and children arrived in the United States between 1900 and 1910 in search of a better life.

America was in the midst of transforming from a nation of farms, shops, and mills into a booming industrial power with factories that needed workers. Major cities, especially in the Northeast and Midwest, bustled with the energy of newly arrived immigrants. Adding to the exploding population of cities were hundreds of thousands of native-born, rural American migrants who were drawn to the cities for the same reasons as foreign immigrants—for better economic opportunities. In 1900, only 40 percent of America's nearly seventy-six million people lived in urban areas. By the end of the decade, 45 percent of the nation's population, which had grown to almost

Connecting the World

As the twentieth century dawned, people finally were able to communicate quickly with those around the world. Telegraph communication across land had been a reality for most people for some time, but sending messages to other continents was not a possibility until telegraph cable had been installed to run across every major ocean. That project was completed in 1902.

Soon, a new invention would replace the telegraph. Italian inventor Guglielmo Marconi (*above*) designed a device to transmit signals through the air and another device to receive them. Marconi's wireless invention was called radio. At first, Marconi was able to send radio signals only over short distances. In December 1901, however, he successfully sent a message from England to Canada. Before long, ships at sea began using radio to communicate with other ships and with people on shore. Radio would continue to flourish for years to come. In the 1920s, the first radio stations began playing music, sports, and news.

ninety-two million, lived in cities. The day would soon come when America's urban population would outnumber the rural population.

San Francisco Earthquake

Early on the morning of April 18, 1906, a horrifying earthquake struck California. The quake was centered near San Francisco, but tremors were felt hundreds of miles away, even in the states of Oregon and Nevada. In San Francisco, buildings tumbled to the ground and fires started throughout the city. Firefighters had no water to stop the blazes with because the quake had broken the city's water lines. The fires burned for three days.

In the end, 80 percent of the city was destroyed. More than three thousand people died in the earthquake and fires. A quarter of a million people were homeless. Little was left but rubble. Eventually San Francisco would be rebuilt. However, many people did not wait for that to happen and instead went south to Los Angeles. The arrival of San Franciscans helped Los Angeles become the most populous city in California. Even today, the 1906 San Francisco earthquake ranks as one of the worst natural disasters in US history.

Writer Jack London referred to the second night of fires devouring San Francisco as "this night of terror." On the night of April 19, London was amazed that people were calm and quiet "while the whole city crashed and roared into ruin." He remarked that the people were kinder and more courteous than at any other time in the city's history.

Hostility Toward Immigrants

The majority of immigrants arriving in the United States during the 1900s were from eastern, central, and southern Europe. A smaller number of Asian immigrants from China and Japan settled in the West, mainly in California. As more immigrants arrived, growing numbers of native-born Americans began to resent the newcomers, who had foreign languages, customs, and religions. They feared that their own language and traditions might be drowned in a sea of strange new cultures. They were also afraid that the new arrivals would take their jobs away because immigrants were willing to work for lower pay.

Probably the worst example of hostility toward immigrants involved Japanese Americans in California. In October 1906, a San Francisco school board voted to segregate (separate by race) Japanese students even though only ninety-three out of twenty-five thousand students in San Francisco were Japanese. The Japanese government complained to US president Theodore Roosevelt when it learned of the situation. Some American politicians were outraged at the Japanese complaint and urged a declaration of war against Japan. To calm the situation and avoid war, President Roosevelt persuaded the school board to end its policy in 1907. However, he first had to work out a so-called Gentlemen's Agreement with the Japanese government, whereby Japan would no longer allow laborers to immigrate to the United States.

Racism in America

During the first decade of the twentieth century, some Americans struggled valiantly to overcome racism—the terrible discrimination that still afflicted the nation almost half a century after the end of slavery. Many immigrant groups were the victims of various forms of discrimination, especially the Chinese and Japanese people on the West coast. But those who suffered the most were American Indians and African Americans.

Over the years, mining companies and land speculators had taken away much of the land that had been promised to American Indians by government treaties. Meanwhile in the South, segregation was the order of the day. Jim Crow laws separated African Americans from

Many Italian immigrants settled in New York City's Little Italy.

Henry Ford and Mass Production

Henry Ford used a method called mass production to keep his factories running smoothly. This method makes it possible to manufacture large quantities of a product at a low cost. A key feature of mass production is the assembly line. On Ford's assembly line, each worker added a part as an unfinished car rolled past. By the time a Model T reached the end of the line, it was finished. At its peak, Ford's assembly line produced a new car every three minutes.

Henry Ford's methods were so efficient that the price of his car actually went down. By 1916, a new Model T cost just $360. Soon, half of all the cars on American roads were Model Ts. Many other companies copied Ford's methods. Mass production is still widely used today.

whites in almost all public facilities, including schools and restrooms. Certain laws, such as voting requirements, were also put into place to ensure that African Americans would not be allowed to vote. Even worse, African Americans were often the victims of brutal violence at the hands of white racists. During the 1900s, one hundred African Americans were lynched, or killed as punishment for an alleged crime without first having a trial.

Two African-American leaders were determined to fight for equality and put an end to discrimination. But these leaders differed in their ideas about the best way to achieve these goals. Booker T. Washington, head of the Tuskegee Institute in Alabama, believed in following the path of least resistance. He believed that African Americans should first help each other to better themselves economically by becoming educated and starting their own businesses. Only then would African Americans have a good chance of winning social and political equality. W. E. B. Du Bois, on the other hand, believed that African Americans should not wait to struggle for equality. He urged African Americans to immediately demand social equality and the protection of the law against segregation and violence. In 1909, to help further these goals, Du Bois and a group of progressive white and black reformers founded the National Association for the Advancement of Colored People (NAACP).

The Economic Climate

America's new role as a global power contributed greatly to an amazing period of growth in the nation's economy. New sources of cheap raw materials were now available to fuel the nation's industries. American corporations also had vast new markets in which to sell and distribute their goods. In such a favorable economic climate, financing was readily available for the creation of new businesses. Millions of job seekers, both foreign immigrants and native-born Americans, also helped boost the economy.

New Forms of Transportation

New methods of transportation played an important role in the growth of America's cities. People rode electric streetcars to get around town. Often, cities grew up around streetcar routes as they were planned and built. The expansion of Los Angeles was accomplished in such a fashion.

While the streetcar was the most popular means of urban transportation, underground travel also became possible during the 1900s. In New York City, the world's largest subway system was completed in 1904.

This image from 1904 shows the construction of the New York City subway system. The construction method used was known as cut and cover.

Mayor Seth Low dedicates the New York City subway.

Americans enjoyed seeking thrills at amusement parks.

But it was the development of the automobile that caused the most excitement during the decade. In 1900, there were about eight thousand registered cars. Fifty manufacturers were selling different forms of the vehicle that was often called the horseless carriage. These vehicles, which were built by hand, cost around one thousand dollars. They were far too expensive for most Americans. That changed when Henry Ford introduced his mass-produced Model T in 1908. The price was $850—well within reach for some middle-class families. Ten thousand Model T Fords were sold during the first year of production. By the decade's end, most of the companies manufacturing horseless carriages at the beginning of the 1900s no longer existed. Because of the enormous technological innovations and price difference, the automobile industry would soon be dominated by Ford, General Motors, and Chrysler.

Amusement Parks

America's love affair with the automobile was just beginning in the 1900s. During these years, Americans also enjoyed other kinds of rides—specifically, amusement park rides, such as the roller coaster. Amusement parks sprang up all across the country and became wildly popular. The parks were easily accessible and affordable, even for working-class Americans.

In New York City, people could ride the streetcar to Coney Island, a resort by the sea, for five cents. Coney Island was home to the world's first roller coaster, known as the Switchback Railroad. It had opened in 1884. Thrill seekers had a choice of several roller coasters, including the famous Loop the Loop, as well as other types of rides, such as a giant Ferris wheel. At Steeplechase Park, visitors lined up to ride mechanical horses that traveled around a circular track high above the park.

Making Household Chores Easier

During the 1900s, many people lived in cramped tenement apartments with few comforts. Only the wealthy and middle class had indoor plumbing. But changes were afoot that would benefit even working-class Americans.

Electricity was becoming available to more people, which made possible the advent of electric household appliances. The electric vacuum cleaner was patented in 1907. At first, only the wealthy could afford one, but eventually, as with other new inventions, the price came down low enough so that almost anyone could afford to buy a vacuum cleaner.

There were many other signs of progress. The icebox provided a practical way to refrigerate food in the home. And thanks to improvements in the canning process, it was no longer necessary for homemakers to can their own food. Canned foods were now available in stores, and even the poor could afford them. Especially popular were the canned products of the Campbell's company.

Probably the most exhausting chore for housewives was the never-ending task of washing clothes. During the 1900s, it became possible to send clothes out to laundries. Little by little, some of the drudgery of household chores was being alleviated.

Rise of Advertising

As a greater variety of household products became available, businesses had to persuade consumers to buy them. Advertising agencies sprang up to spread the word. An effective way of reaching the greatest number of people was through the placing of advertisements in the pages of popular magazines, such as the *Saturday Evening Post*. Advertising copywriters came up with catchy phrases. For example, "Milk From Contented Cows" promoted Carnation's dairy products.

St. Louis World's Fair

Every year, the World's Fair showed off new inventions and ideas. In 1904, the city of St. Louis, Missouri, hosted the fair, which lasted seven months and drew nearly 20 million attendees. The fair's 1,500 exhibits featured new advances in science and industry. There were also musical concerts, stage plays, and carnival rides.

Most visitors needed at least a week to see the entire fair. President Theodore Roosevelt went twice. Several new food items were unveiled at the St. Louis World's Fair. These included peanut butter, cotton candy, iced tea, and the waffle-style ice cream cone.

The fair brought money and prestige to its host city. At the time, St. Louis was the fourth-largest city in the United States. By the time the fair closed in December 1904, its profits had reached $25 million. Today, that amount would equal more than half a billion dollars.

Named after President Theodore Roosevelt, the teddy bear would become a national fad. More than two hundred years later, its popularity has not waned.

The Teddy Bear

It all started when President Theodore Roosevelt went on a hunting trip in November 1902. Although he was an experienced hunter, he was not having any luck. So members of his party caught a young bear and tied it to a tree. The president, however, refused to shoot it—doing so would have gone against his idea of good sportsmanship. When word of this incident spread, it became the subject of cartoons in the newspapers.

Morris and Rose Mitchom, an enterprising couple who owned a candy store in Brooklyn, New York, began selling a toy bear with moveable body parts. Rose had stitched together the original bear by hand. The Mitchoms received permission from the president to call their product Teddy's bear. Because of the publicity about the incident,

the bears sold like hotcakes. The Mitchoms could not keep up with the demand, so they teamed up with the Butler Brothers. Together, they started the Ideal Novelty and Toy Company to mass-produce and market their Teddy's bear, whose name would later be changed to teddy bear. The following year, the Teddy Bear craze swept across America. It lasted at least until the end of Roosevelt's second term in office in 1909.

Victorian Fashion

Great Britain's Queen Victoria died on January 22, 1901, but the Victorian influence on fashion in America would continue for most of the 1900s. For women of the upper and middle classes, this meant another decade of formality that was characterized by the S-shaped silhouette. This look was achieved by draping a long bell-shaped skirt over stiff, ruffled petticoats that covered the shoes. At the back, a small, heavy bustle gathered a cloth train. A corset laced as tightly as possible forced a tiny waist and flat stomach while exaggerating the breasts and bustled hips. Completing the look was a high and stiff collar, a wide-brimmed hat, and pointed suede shoes or leather boots fastened with buttons.

By the end of the decade, formality was declining. Women were getting tired of always being uncomfortable. Hemlines rose to the top of the boot, skirts narrowed slightly, corsets no longer reached above the waist, and petticoats were replaced by closer-fitting slips.

Ready-to-Wear Clothing

Another fashion trend had emerged during the 1890s in the illustrations of Charles Dana Gibson, whose work appeared in the pages of *Life* magazine. The Gibson look became increasingly popular with American women during the 1900s. It featured the shirtwaist—a

During the 1900s, women wore corsets and long skirts, but gradually waists would be loosened and hemlines would rise.

blouse designed to be worn with a high-waisted ankle-length skirt. Young women who aspired to be secretaries or typists were often drawn to the Gibson looks, as they favored practical, comfortable, yet stylish clothing that could be worn for everyday activities, especially for work at the office.

Except for the rich, most American women had always made their own clothes. But the influx of Jewish and Eastern European tailors led to the growth of the ready-to-wear clothing industry in New York City. During the 1900s, many women bought shirtwaists and other items from the mail-order Sears, Roebuck catalog. By 1905, the catalog offered one hundred fifty different types of shirtwaists.

Men's Fashion

Like women's fashions during this decade, men's clothing was slowly becoming less stiff and formal. Many young men were moving away from the Victorian full beard. They dared to appear in public with just a mustache or even a totally clean-shaven face. In 1901, middle- and upper-class men typically wore a long frock coat, a waistcoat, and striped trousers to the office. They wore a closely fitted dinner jacket in the evening. By the middle of the decade, young men began wearing a more relaxed lounge suit to the office. A hat was popular for most occasions, whether it was a silk top hat, a soft felt homburg, a bowler with a rounded top and narrow brim, or a straw hat, known as a boater, which was worn in the summer. Other popular accessories included cuff links and pocket watches with long chains.

Booker T. Washington wore the typical men's fashion of the day.

Comic actor Buster Keaton (1895–1966) performs in his family's vaudeville act in 1905.

Entertainment and the Arts

The 1900s were a decade of new entertainments. Vaudeville thrived and began to give way to early movies. Americans enjoyed sitting around the piano playing popular music and listening to recordings on phonographs. New musical forms, such as ragtime and the blues, were beginning to take root. Art moved into a new period. While some of the artistic offerings of the decade were good old-fashioned entertainment, much of it had a social conscience.

The Jungle

Novelist Upton Sinclair was known as a muckraker, a name given to those who exposed corruption (in other words, raked up the muck) in business or politics. Sinclair had earned the title by writing an exposé of the meatpacking industry in his novel *The Jungle*, published in 1906. The characters in the novel were poor immigrants from Lithuania who worked in Chicago's stockyards and meat-processing plants. Sinclair filled his realistic portrayal with graphic descriptions of the extremely unsanitary practices that were used in the meat industry.

When President Theodore Roosevelt read the book, he was outraged by what was going on in Chicago. He ordered Congress to do something about it. After government investigators confirmed that Sinclair's description was true, Congress passed the Pure Food and Drug Act and the Meat Inspection Act. Roosevelt signed both into law on the same day.

Still, Upton Sinclair was not totally satisfied. He had hoped to improve the lot of poor workers in the meat-processing plants by drawing attention to their awful working conditions as well as the unsanitary practices. Americans, however, were more concerned about their own food. "I aimed for the public's heart and by accident I hit it in the stomach," Sinclair said.

Helen Keller

Helen Keller had been blind and deaf since she was nineteen months old. When Helen was six, her tutor, Anne Sullivan, taught her how to spell words by tracing the shapes of letters onto Helen's hand. One day, Sullivan wrote "water" on Helen's hand while pouring water from a pump onto Helen's other hand. Only then did Helen grasp that the words she had been spelling were the names of things and that everything has a name.

Helen soon learned hundreds of words and then learned how to read using braille, a system of reading for the blind. Helen wrote poems and stories. By the time she was ten, Helen was communicating with sign language. By age sixteen, she had learned to speak by touching people's noses, lips, and throats as they spoke to her. In 1902, Helen became famous when her autobiography, *The Story of My Life*, was published. In 1904, she graduated from Radcliffe College. She was twenty-two years old. She then devoted her time to improving education for the blind and deaf.

Upton Sinclair

During his lifetime, Upton Sinclair (1878–1968) wrote more than ninety books. His 1943 novel *Dragon's Teeth* won the Pulitzer Prize. Some of his other books explored the conditions that workers faced in industries other than meatpacking, such as coal mining, oil drilling, and auto manufacturing.

Blind and deaf since childhood, Helen Keller learned to read Braille and to communicate using sign language.

The Twelve-Minute Western

Americans had begun viewing moving pictures in the 1890s. While looking into a machine known as a kinetoscope, they turned a crank with their hand. The figures on the tiny screen seemed to come to life before their eyes. But after the novelty wore off, audiences grew tired of the silent newsreels and sight gags that typically lasted about half a minute. Soon, however, movies took a major leap forward.

In 1903, Edwin Porter produced a twelve-minute-long silent film called *The Great Train Robbery*. The plot was inspired by a

This scene is from the highly successful silent film *The Great Train Robbery*. Americans flocked to theaters to watch Western motion pictures.

The Phonograph

During his life, Thomas Edison created more than a thousand inventions, including the first practical electric light and a motion picture camera. Edison also invented a machine called the phonograph, which allowed people to listen to recorded music. Before Edison's invention, people had to go to a concert or other live performance to hear music.

Edison's phonograph was an early form of the record player. The records it played were fragile and broke easily. People did not let that stop them from owning phonographs. For the first time, they could hear fine music at home. Edison was surprised that people used his invention for music. He thought it would be better used for office work.

real event—a train robbery committed by Butch Cassidy and his gang in Wyoming in August 1900. *The Great Train Robbery* was America's first Western movie. Audiences were thrilled to see gunslingers of the Old West galloping across the screen. They were captivated by the conflict between heroes and villains.

Like all other movies of the time, the film was in black and white and had no sound. However, it showed movie companies that people liked serious films. Soon the public began clamoring for more movies. More Westerns followed, as well as Civil War dramas, crime stories, and comedies. But *The Great Train Robbery* remained the single most popular movie of the decade. Eventually, movies became longer and more exciting with the addition of sound and color.

From the Stage to Movies

At first, films were shown as part of the entertainment at vaudeville theaters between the live acts. Vaudeville entertainment featured singers, dancers, comedians, acrobats, and jugglers. Among the most famous vaudeville entertainers were Bert Williams, an African-American singer and dancer; Eddie Foy, an Irish dancer and pantomimist; comedian Ed Wynn; and singers Sophie Tucker and Al Jolson. There were also novelty acts, such as Blatz the Human Fish, who ate, read, and played the trombone under water. Also popular was female impersonator Julian Eltinge, who in 1907 dressed up as the Simpson Girl, a spoof of the Gibson girl look.

Films were also shown in storefronts with the audience on folding chairs in front of a screen. In 1905, one such theater with comfortable seating and live piano accompaniment opened in Pittsburgh, Pennsylvania. Admission was a nickel, and the theater became known as a nickelodeon. Vaudeville remained popular through

Comedian and actor Ed Wynn began his entertainment career in Vaudeville. He hosted a popular radio show and, much later, appeared in film and television.

the first decade of the twentieth century, but movies gradually started to replace it. By 1909, there were more than four thousand nickelodeons in America, and more than eighty million tickets were being sold every week.

Sheet Music

One evening in 1903, a New York City newspaper reporter was strolling down Twenty-Eighth Street in Manhattan. When he entered the

Millions of Americans visited nickelodeons every week.

block between Broadway and Sixth Avenue, he heard a confusion of musical sounds coming at him from open windows on both sides of the street. He was overwhelmed by the effect of clashing melodies and harmonies. Upon investigating the situation, the reporter learned that up and down the block, the offices were occupied by publishers of sheet music. In each building, songwriters and piano players were hard at work cranking out new songs. The reporter called the street Tin Pan Alley because of all the noise.

There was a lot of money to be made from selling sheet music, especially if the songs became popular hits. Music was common entertainment in the homes of many Americans, and many families owned a piano. Phonographs and records were also becoming popular. At first, most recorded music consisted of excerpts from operas featuring famous singers, such as Enrico Caruso. By the end of the decade, popular songs found their way onto phonograph records. Among the decade's most popular tunes were "In the Good Old Summertime" (1902), "Meet Me in St. Louis" (1904), and "Give My Regards to Broadway" (1904).

Syncopated Rhythms

A style of music known as ragtime was especially popular throughout the decade. It originated in the 1880s as an African-American musical form featuring syncopated rhythms. The ragtime piano compositions of African-American pianist Scott Joplin became known for their distinctive melodies and rich harmonies. Joplin soon came to be called the Ragtime King. His "Maple Leaf Rag," composed in 1899, became America's most popular piano rag by 1909. However, not everyone in America was fond of ragtime music. In 1901, the American Federation of Musicians passed an anti-ragtime resolution calling for "every effort to suppress and discourage such musical trash." Despite these efforts, ragtime thrived.

Scott Joplin (1867–1917) was a pioneer of the style of music known as ragtime. His "Maple Leaf Rag" is considered the archetype of ragtime music.

The Blues

Since the days of slavery, African Americans in the South had been singing the blues—songs of sorrow, loneliness, defiance, and humor. The typical format of a blues song was a 12-bar melody with repeats and responses. Ma Rainey (born Gertrude Pridgett), an African-American singer, heard her first blues song in 1902. Ma Rainey performed in minstrel shows, a type of variety entertainment that had been popular since the Civil War. When she began singing blues songs on stage, she became known as the Mother of the Blues. W.C. Handy, known as the Father of the Blues, wrote his first blues song in 1909. In the years to come, the blues and ragtime would be the main elements of a new music called jazz.

Picasso and Modern Art

The first decade of the twentieth century brought big changes to the art world. There were new styles and subjects. In the past, artists had focused on scenes from nature, history, or mythology. By 1900, modern art had arrived. Paintings were more vivid and expressed thought, feeling, and emotion.

Pablo Picasso helped define modern art. Picasso dedicated his life to painting. Born in Spain in 1881, he was the son of an art teacher. By the age of twenty, Picasso had created his own style of painting. Using only shades of blue, he created touching scenes of poverty and sadness. In 1904, Picasso's Blue Period gave way to his Rose Period. He used red colors to portray circus performers and other entertainers.

Later in the decade, Picasso started painting strange abstract shapes. His work featured sharp angles and flat planes. He created images that were impossible in real life. The style came to be known as cubism. Picasso's new method was so radical that even some of his fellow artists disapproved. Regardless, his brilliance was eventually recognized. He inspired future generations of artists. Today, Picasso's paintings hang in the world's best museums.

Pablo Picasso created the style of painting known as cubism.

Sports

As a child, President Theodore Roosevelt had suffered from asthma and spent most of his time indoors. As he grew older, his father encouraged him to participate in strenuous sports, such as boxing, swimming, and horseback riding, to regain his health. President Roosevelt's love of sports had tremendous influence over Americans, who found themselves with leisure time to pursue sports thanks to the Industrial Revolution.

The Dangerous Game of Football

One of President Roosevelt's favorite sports was football. He admired the aggressive behavior on the playing field. The only problem was that football, especially college football, was extremely brutal during the 1900s. Many young men were killed while playing. Eventually, pressure grew to find a way to make football less dangerous. Some journalists and college presidents were even calling for the game to be abolished.

In 1905, Roosevelt called a football summit before the start of the college football season. He invited athletic officials and presidents of the Ivy League colleges to the White House. Roosevelt thought he could persuade them to "teach men to play football honestly."

Racing Takes Root

Automobile racing began in Europe in 1894. It quickly caught on in the United States. Early races ran along country roads. In 1909, the famous Indianapolis Motor Speedway opened. Afterward, oval-track racing became the standard in America. The average speed of early races was only about 75 miles per hour. Today's race cars speed by at 240 miles per hour! Auto racing has become incredibly popular and very lucrative in America today.

College football, however, had become a huge commercial enterprise. Winning meant everything—a college's prestige depended on victory. Training was often haphazard with punishing schedules. At times, violence was deliberately encouraged.

Very little was accomplished at the White House summit. The delegates promised to "eliminate unnecessary roughness, holding, and foul play." On the playing field, however, nothing changed. During the 1905 season, eighteen players died and 159 were seriously injured. The next year, two organizations—the Intercollegiate Athletic Association (IAA) and the Intercollegiate Rules Committee—joined to make some changes in the rules of the game to reduce the brutality of football. Still, players continued to die. There was no significant

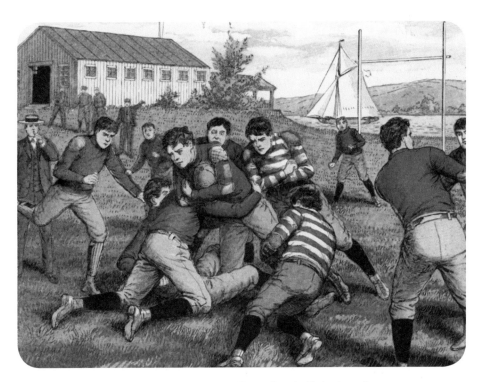

Injuries and deaths were rampant in college football during the 1900s. Protective equipment wouldn't be introduced until the next decade.

drop in the death and injury rate until protective equipment was introduced during the 1910s.

Changes in Baseball

By 1900, baseball had been popular with American sports lovers for at least a quarter of a century. The National League (NL), in existence since 1876, had eight teams in 1900—Boston, Brooklyn, Chicago, Cincinnati, New York, Philadelphia, Pittsburgh, and St. Louis. Although baseball had been around for quite a while, changes were coming.

In 1900, Byron Bancroft "Ban" Johnson, the president of the minor-league Western Association (WA), announced that he was changing the league's name to the American League (AL). It would now be considered a major league on the same level as the NL.

At first, NL officials did not take the AL seriously. But once they realized that baseball fans were very interested in the new league, they became concerned. They soon saw that the AL meant trouble for the NL. By 1903, more than one hundred NL players, many of them popular with the fans, had switched to the AL in response to offers of better salaries.

Something had to be done. In 1903, managers from the two leagues got together and hammered out an agreement called the Joint Playing Rules. These became the official rules of baseball for both leagues. Then, they scheduled a special baseball event, a World Series, which would take place at the close of the 1903 baseball season. The champion teams of each league would play in a five-out-of-nine series. In the 1903 World Series, the NL's Pittsburgh Pirates played against the AL's Boston Pilgrims. To the surprise of the NL, Boston won. The following year, in 1904, there was no World Series. The NL's champion team, the New York Giants, refused to play Boston, which was once again the AL's champion. Giants manager John McGraw refused to play against what he called a "minor league" club. Perhaps

Cy Young (1867–1955)

Baseball fans went wild for the first World Series. Some went to see every game. They traveled by train between Boston and Pittsburgh. The Boston team had a great pitcher named Cy Young. Boston won five of the eight games played and became the first World Series champions.

Cy Young had an outstanding season in 1903. He won twenty-eight games and lost only nine. Young pitched from 1890 to 1911 and won 511 games during his career. This is more than any other pitcher in baseball history. The Cy Young Award is awarded every year to to the best major league pitcher.

Henri Herouin won the gold in archery at the 1900 Paris Olympics.

he had another reason—a fear of losing. At any rate, baseball fans were disappointed. So, in 1905, both leagues once again held a World Series. This time, it would be a four-out-of-seven series. The New York Giants defeated the AL's Philadelphia Athletics. From then on, the World Series would be an important annual event to the delight of baseball fans all across America.

The Olympics

Three Olympic Games were held during the first decade of the twentieth century. However, since the Olympics did not yet occur every four years as they do today, there was some irregularity.

American Maxwell Long won the gold medal for the 400-meter race in the 1900 Paris Olympic Games.

In 1900, the second modern Olympic Games competition was held in Paris, France. (The first modern Games had taken place in 1896 after a break of fifteen hundred years since the last Olympics.) Although many of the athletes from other nations found the behavior of the American team somewhat loud and rude—the French called the Americans *sauvages* (savages)—the Games were marked by a friendly and warm spirit of sportsmanship.

The United States athletes dominated the Games in track and field events, particularly in sprints. Among the big winners was American J.W.B. Tewksbury, who ran to victory in the 200-meter dash. Strangely, the University of Pennsylvania student Tewksbury and many of his teammates did not realize that the competition was, in fact, the Olympics until they were handed medals!

The third Olympic Games were held in St. Louis, Missouri, at the same time as the World's Fair. The Games drew more than six hundred athletes from twelve countries. However, most of the athletes were American. A special event known as the Intercalated Games was held in 1906 in Athens. These games are not officially recognized today by the International Olympic Committee. In 1908, the advent of the traditional four-year cycle, the fourth Olympic Games were held in London. These games lasted six months!

National and International Politics

On September 6, 1901, President McKinley was assassinated while attending the Pan-American Exposition in Buffalo, New York. He was shot by Leon Czolgosz, a man claiming to be an anarchist, or someone who opposes all government. Vice President Theodore Roosevelt became president.

American Forces Go Abroad

For many years, the United States stayed out of world events. Americans cared little about what other countries did. By 1900, that was no longer true. US troops were going overseas. American forces helped put down an uprising in China. By the beginning of the twentieth century, China had lost a series of wars. Foreign countries took advantage of its weak government and forced China to trade with them in ways that did not benefit the Chinese. They also forced China to allow foreign citizens to live in the country. In 1900, a group known as the Boxers started attacking foreigners in an effort to rid China of all foreign influences. Troops from Great Britain, Germany, France, Japan, and several other countries sailed for China to stop the Boxers. President William McKinley sent 2,500 US sailors and marines to join this effort. McKinley wanted the United States to get its share of trade with

This illustration shows European diplomats being freed after the Boxer Rebellion.

In September 1901, just six months into his term as president, William McKinley was shot by anarchist Leon Czolgosz. McKinley died days later.

China. The Americans and their allies fought their way to the capital city of Beijing by August 1900. By September of the following year, the Boxer Rebellion had been crushed.

Roosevelt's Journey to the Presidency

Roosevelt's ascension to the White House began a period of presidential politics known as the Progressive Era, which would last for almost two decades. The forty-two-year-old Republican president was eager to tackle difficult challenges and accomplish great things.

Roosevelt had previously served as a New York state assemblyman. In the assembly, he had stood up to wealthy railroad owner Jay Gould and had sponsored legislation to improve the working conditions

McKinley's Assassination

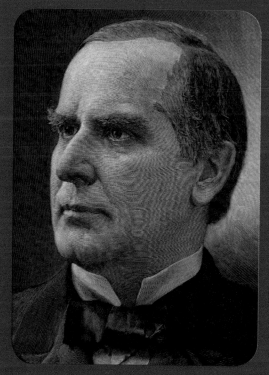

William McKinley (1843–1901) was elected president of the United States as the Republican Party's candidate in 1896. McKinley won a large majority in the electoral college that year with 271 electoral votes to 176 for the Democratic Party candidate, William Jennings Bryan. In 1900, McKinley was reelected by an even wider margin over Bryan, 292 electoral votes to 155.

On September 6, 1901, a man named Leon Czolgosz shot President McKinley in a public hall at the Pan-American Exposition in Buffalo, New York. Czolgosz was an anarchist, or a person who wants to do away with the government. At 4:07 p.m., Czolgosz fired two shots from a .32 caliber revolver at the president. One bullet hit McKinley's ribs. The other passed through McKinley's stomach, colon, and kidney and lodged in his back. Czolgosz was immediately tackled and arrested. The wounded president was quickly taken to a hospital. There, doctors removed one bullet. However, they felt it would cause too much damage to try to find the second bullet, so they closed McKinley's wounds. At first, it appeared that McKinley would recover from the shooting. However, on September 12 his health took a turn for the worse. At 2:15 a.m. on September 14, William McKinley died from infection and gangrene caused by his wounds.

of New York City cigar makers. Later, as a New York City police commissioner, he worked to clean up a corrupt city police force.

In 1896, Roosevelt was appointed Assistant Secretary of the Navy by President McKinley. At that time, Cubans were trying to win their freedom from Spain. Roosevelt was in favor of helping the Cubans. Because McKinley did not want to risk war with Spain, the outspoken Roosevelt declared that McKinley had "no more backbone than a chocolate eclair." War finally did break out between the United States and Spain in February 1898, after the American battleship *Maine* blew up in a Cuban harbor.

Roosevelt left his navy job and volunteered for the Army. He trained for a month with a one-thousand-man regiment made up of cowboys, frontiersmen, and an assortment of sportsmen who became known as Roosevelt's Rough Riders. In Cuba, he led his troops against the Spaniards in a famous charge up San Juan Hill, near the city of Santiago. Also taking part in the battle was the 10th cavalry regiment of African-American troops. Roosevelt regarded his experience at San Juan Hill as "the great day of my life."

The Spanish-American War of 1898 was over in just six months. The victorious United States won control of the former Spanish possessions of Cuba and Puerto Rico in the Caribbean and the Philippines, Guam, and Wake Island in the Pacific. Later that year, Roosevelt, now considered a war hero, was elected Governor of New York. Two years later, the Republicans chose him as McKinley's vice presidential running mate in the election of 1900. After McKinley's assassination, President Roosevelt, the enthusiastic Rough Rider, was ready for new battles.

Fighting the Trusts

The purpose of the Sherman Antitrust Act of 1890 was to prevent businesses from joining together in ways that would restrain trade

Railroad magnates formed monopolies to gain unfair advantages.

or commerce. Unfortunately, the government did not enforce the act. The most powerful corporations in industries such as railroads, aluminum, tobacco, life insurance, sugar, and coal gobbled up weaker competitors and merged with strong competitors to form huge monopolies known as trusts.

In 1900, President McKinley had campaigned against the trusts. He said they were "dangerous conspiracies against the public good" and that they should be regulated by law. Theodore Roosevelt agreed. In his first State of the Union Address, he argued that because the trusts did business in many states, they could not be regulated by state law. The federal government had to "assume the power of supervision and regulation over all corporations doing an interstate business."

The arrogant attitude and blatant disregard for the public good shown by one of America's wealthiest men, John Pierpont (J. P.) Morgan, particularly infuriated Roosevelt. Morgan had once commented, "I owe the public nothing." He explained that it was his duty to bring rival companies together in a trust for their mutual benefit. He claimed to want to make business more rational and efficient. Many of his critics, however, believed he and his associates were instead working to cheat the public. In 1902, the Roosevelt administration brought a suit under the Sherman Antitrust Act to dissolve the Northern Securities Company, a transportation monopoly controlled by Morgan.

In 1903, Congress agreed to Roosevelt's proposal to create the Department of Commerce and Labor, including a Bureau of Corporations to investigate possible violations of antitrust law. In 1904, the Supreme Court ordered that Northern Securities be dissolved. When William Howard Taft, Roosevelt's handpicked successor, became president in 1909, he continued the antitrust suits brought by Roosevelt. Indeed, Taft would prove to be an even more effective trustbuster than Roosevelt.

Ending the Coal Strike

In 1902, Theodore Roosevelt became the first president to mediate a labor dispute. About one hundred fifty thousand mine workers in the Northeast, led by John Mitchell, president of the United Mine Workers (UMW), went on strike for better pay, a shorter workday, and recognition of their union. During the next few months, the price of coal skyrocketed as supplies dwindled. With winter approaching, Roosevelt was determined to take action to end the strike.

Roosevelt used his power as president to break the standoff. He invited the mine owners to Washington, D.C. He also asked the leaders of the miners to come. The mine owners had refused to negotiate with the union. They demanded that Roosevelt send in troops to crush the strike. By this time, most of the American public sympathized with the miners. Angered by the mine owners' stubbornness, Roosevelt threatened to send in the Army—not to attack the miners but to seize and operate the mines. This sent the mine owners scurrying to the negotiating table, and the five-month-long anthracite coal strike was called off. At the mediation session in Scranton, Pennsylvania, both sides agreed to a 10 percent pay increase for the miners and a nine-hour workday.

The mines were once again running with plenty of coal to heat homes and businesses during the winter. Roosevelt had not only solved the crisis, but he also showed business owners and workers how to compromise and resolve their differences.

Digging the Panama Canal

In 1903, the United States wanted to build a canal across Panama, which was then a province of Colombia. For many years, the only ways to travel by water from the Atlantic to the Pacific were to either sail around the tip of South America or to sail to Central America, cross overland, and then take another ship on the Pacific side. A canal

Americans lined up to buy coal during the coal strike of 1902.

Feats of Ingenuity

American leaders took advantage of France's failures when building the Panama Canal. A French company had first tried to dig a canal through Panama in the late 1800s. Cutting through the country's steep mountains and surviving the wet climate proved too challenging. After almost ten years of work, the French company gave up.

First, American leaders did their best to make sure workers stayed healthy. A US Army doctor named William Gorgas (*above*) found that two of the deadliest tropical diseases—yellow fever and malaria—were spread by mosquito bites. Gorgas ordered chemicals to be sprayed on mosquito breeding areas to kill the insects. He also helped keep tens of thousands of workers from getting ill by making sure that they had plenty of clean water to drink.

American engineers avoided another mistake the French had made. Instead of trying to cut through mountains to build the entire canal at sea level, they decided to build a series of locks to raise ships over the high ground. This network of locks allows ships to climb steep terrain.

would dramatically shorten the trip by providing ships with a water route through Central America.

Colombia did not agree to the United States' proposal to build a canal, however. Encouraged by the United States, Panamanians made plans to secede from, or leave, Colombia. When Colombia sent troops to stop the Panamanians, US Navy ships prevented them from landing. The US government recognized Panama's independence, and a grateful Panama gave the United States a ten-mile-wide strip of land across Panama on which to build a canal.

Construction on the fifty-one-mile-long Panama Canal began shortly after the signing of the agreement between the two countries. It would take ten years to complete before it opened in 1914. There were many landslides and accidents during construction, and more

Construction of the Panama Canal reduced travel time by six weeks. This feat of engineering was an important development for the shipping industry.

Japan's Newly Built Military

From the 1600s to the mid-1800s, Japanese leaders had kept their country isolated. During that time, the Industrial Revolution had transformed much of the world, but it was unknown in Japan. As a result, Japan had fallen far behind other nations. In the late 1800s, Japanese leaders decided their country needed to catch up. In an effort to make Japan a modern country as quickly as possible, they imported Western technology, brought in foreign experts, and built better schools. They also built a powerful army and navy. Japanese leaders were eager to prove that these efforts had worked. The war against Russia was Japan's chance to test its new military strength.

than five thousand workers died on the job. But the canal's opening made it possible for ships to travel between the Atlantic and the Pacific in less than ten hours rather than five or six weeks. For decades, the Panama Canal was run by the United States. In 1999, the United States turned over control to Panama. Today, more than fourteen thousand ships pass through the Panama Canal each year. Each ship saves thousands of miles on its journey. Building the Panama Canal was one of the greatest feats in human history.

Presidential Election

When Roosevelt ran for another term in office in 1904, he promised Americans a Square Deal. Mindful of Roosevelt's intervention in the coal strike and his breakup of Northern Securities, many believed in his sense of fairness. Americans also responded favorably when Roosevelt advocated the conservation of natural resources on public land. He was the first president to do so. Believing Roosevelt had their best interests at heart, Americans voted him into office for a full term of his own.

Roosevelt had a number of firsts during his presidency. In 1906, he became the first president to win the Nobel Peace Prize, which he received for his role as mediator in helping to end the 1904–1905 war between Russia and Japan. In 1906, Roosevelt traveled to Panama to see for himself how the Panama Canal project was progressing, thus becoming the first president to take a trip abroad. In 1910, the year after he left office, Roosevelt was looking for new adventures and went for a ride in a plane built by the Wright brothers.

War Erupts Between Japan and Russia

Roosevelt became associated with a phrase taken from a West African proverb, "Speak softly and carry a big stick." He believed that a policy based on persuasive diplomacy backed by military might was the best way to get things done. Time and again, Roosevelt followed this

Russian artist Vladimir Makovsky captured the desperation of the working poor in this study for his painting titled Bloody Sunday.

principle in his dealings with the nations of the Caribbean and Latin America. In 1902, by announcing that the United States Navy was ready to go into action, he persuaded Germany, Great Britain, and Italy to negotiate with Venezuela over the payment of debts rather than intervene militarily.

President Roosevelt was eager to project American power and influence to more distant parts of the world, as well as in Latin America. In September 1905, he mediated an end to the war between rivals Russia and Japan, which was becoming America's chief rival in the Pacific. The war had begun in February 1904 after tensions between the two nations had reached a boiling point. Each wanted control over Korea and Chinese Manchuria, but it soon became clear that victory was beyond the grasp of either power—although the much smaller Japan was able to humiliate the great Russian Empire by sinking many of its ships.

Russian Massacre

Russia's leader, Tsar Nicholas II, also had to deal with a revolution that swept through Russia in 1905. On January 22, 1905, a day that would become known as Bloody Sunday, some two hundred thousand Russians, mainly poor working people, marched peacefully through St. Petersburg. They had taken to the streets to plead with the Tsar for better working and living conditions. Tsar Nicholas's soldiers met the marchers with a sudden hail of gunfire, which killed hundreds of men, women, and children and wounded thousands more.

The 1905 rebellion by outraged citizens spread throughout Russia. Millions of striking workers brought the nation to a standstill. In his October Manifesto, Nicholas II agreed to grant the Russian people civil rights, including an elected lawmaking body called the Duma. After the revolution ended, however, Nicholas failed to live up to his promises. He dissolved the Duma when it dared to challenge his policies.

The forced relocation of American Indians is called the Trail of Tears.

Battleship World Tour

In 1907, Theodore Roosevelt sent the Great White Fleet, a group of sixteen United States battleships so named because of their color, on a 43,000-mile (69,202-kilometer) world tour. Among the places the fleet visited were Japan, China, and Australia. The tour was designed to show the world the terrific naval power of the United States and to intimidate those nations that might consider challenging American interests abroad. As a result of the fleet's trip, the United States and Japan signed a new agreement spelling out their mutual interests in the Pacific Ocean. Japan was permitted to keep Korea in return for recognizing American rule over the Philippines, which the United States had won from Spain in the Spanish-American War of 1898.

Oklahoma Becomes a State

In 1907, Oklahoma became the forty-sixth state. For some, this was a happy event, but for American Indians it was the end of a long and tragic story. During the 1800s, America grew rapidly. As white settlers moved west, they took ancient tribal lands from American Indians. The United States government uprooted tribes from the southeastern part of the country and forced them to settle in an area of present-day Oklahoma they called Indian Territory. Tens of thousands of Choctaw, Seminole, Cherokee, and others were moved there. The long journey from their homelands claimed many lives. American Indians remember it as the Trail of Tears. By the 1880s, white settlers wanted land in the Indian Territory. Though it was against the law, whites began moving there, and the tribes slowly disappeared. By 1907, only 9 percent of the people living in Indian Territory were American Indians. Congress granted them US citizenship, and Indian Territory became a candidate for statehood. Some American Indians were against this, but others accepted the change. They helped write the laws that would govern the new state. Oklahoma joined the Union on November 16, 1907.

The NAACP Is Founded

The Civil War (1861–1865) ended slavery in the United States. However, it did not end prejudice and hatred. African Americans were still treated poorly. In 1908, a vicious race riot had broken out in Springfield, Illinois, and several African-American citizens were killed. The riot proved that racism was still a big problem in America.

The following year, a small group of African Americans and whites chose to fight racism by forming the National Association for the Advancement of Colored People (NAACP). More than forty concerned people, led by African-American scholar W. E. B. Du Bois, met in New York City to create the NAACP. Its goal was to promote fair treatment for all Americans.

Since its founding, the NAACP has worked to stop racism. It fought unfair laws designed to keep African Americans from voting. It also fought segregation, which lasted in some Southern states until the 1960s. Today, the NAACP continues to promote equal rights for all.

Civil rights activist
W. E. B. DuBois
cofounded the NAACP.

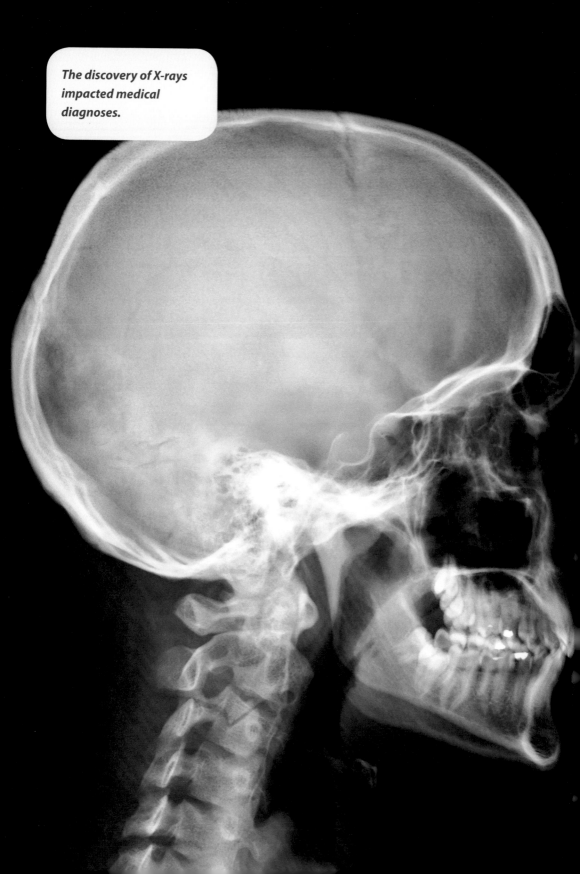

The discovery of X-rays impacted medical diagnoses.

Advances in Science, Technology, and Medicine

Thanks in great part to the momentum created by the Industrial Revolution, the 1900s was a decade of great scientific discoveries. Travel by air was suddenly a possibility. An exploration team finally reached the North Pole. The X-ray improved medical diagnoses. And Albert Einstein would advance the field of physics, although his findings would not be accepted right away. The advances in science, technology, and medicine that took place in this decade would snowball into amazing discoveries throughout the century.

A New Era of Air Travel

Since the beginning of time, people had entertained the idea of someday flying through the air. That fantasy finally became a reality in the first decade of the twentieth century.

On December 17, 1903, at Kitty Hawk, North Carolina, Orville Wright made the first powered flight in a heavier-than-air flying machine he had built with his brother, Wilbur. The flight in the aeroplane, as they called their machine, lasted all of twelve seconds. Orville flew 120 feet (36.5 m) at an average speed of 30 miles (48 km) per hour. The brothers made several other flights that day with one lasting 59 seconds and covering 852 feet (260 m).

The Wright Brothers

The Wrights were an unlikely pair for such a great advance in transportation. Neither one had finished high school. Still, they were good at building machines. As young men in Dayton, Ohio, the Wrights started a bicycle company. Bicycles were fine, but Orville and Wilbur wanted to design other machines.

Around the world, inventors were trying to create a flying machine. The Wrights eagerly read about these attempts. They were fascinated by the work of German inventor Otto Lilienthal. Lilienthal died in 1896, when one of his inventions crashed to the ground. The tragedy taught the Wrights the value of caution. They used kites to experiment before trying to fly on their own. After their successful flight, the Wright brothers became international celebrities.

Orville Wright was not the first person to travel in the air, although he was the first to fly successfully in a heavier-than-air, motor-driven flying machine. Others before had attempted to fly gliders with motors but had failed. Samuel Langley had experimented with unmanned motor-driven model airplanes. He flew a model with a one-horsepower steam engine for one thousand feet along the Potomac River in 1903. Also in 1903, two months before Orville Wright's flight, Charles Manly, attempting to fly an airplane with a five-cylinder engine, had to be pulled from the Potomac River after a crash.

People had also been rising into the sky for many years in balloons, which are lighter-than-air crafts. By 1859, at least three thousand balloon ascents had occurred. In 1900, the first flight of a navigable airship, known as a zeppelin, took place at Lake Constance in Germany. In 1905, Roy Knabenshue flew a sixty-two-foot dirigible over New York City. With the Wright brothers' success, however, a new era of air travel had begun. Whether in an airplane or a dirigible, more people would be able to have a bird's-eye view of the earth below.

Reaching the North Pole

On April 6, 1909, American Commander Robert Edwin Peary became the first person to reach the North Pole. It had been a long campaign involving six earlier expeditions that had failed to reach the pole for one reason or another.

The seventh and final expedition left New York on July 6, 1908. Peary set out with a team of twenty-three men that included Matthew Henson, an African American who helped guide the group during its journey. There were also four Inuit (native to the Arctic region) guides. The team endured bitter cold to travel across frozen plains of shifting ice. Finding the North Pole was difficult because it was just another swath of snow and ice.

When Peary and his team reached the North Pole, the sky was overcast. To verify that he had indeed reached the pole, Peary needed to take readings of the position of the sun. He traveled to a point ten miles away where the sky was clear. There, he made readings of the altitude of the sun with his instruments. He then backtracked to another point eight miles away and again took readings. He did this several times while wandering back and forth across the pole. In his log, he wrote, "I had for all practical purposes passed over the point where north and south and east and west blend into one." When Peary's claim to discovering the North Pole was finally accepted, after some initial skepticism was laid to rest, Peary was promoted to the rank of Rear Admiral by Congress in 1911.

Marie Curie's Research on Radioactivity

Upon learning of Henri Becquerel's discovery of mysterious rays given off by the element uranium, scientist Marie Curie decided to find out more. She called the unknown rays "radiation." Upon experimenting with samples of uranium and pitchblende, a mineral, she discovered that pitchblende was far more radioactive than uranium. She and her husband, Pierre, discovered two new elements in the pitchblende— polonium, named after Marie's native Poland, and radium. In 1903, Marie Curie became the first woman to be awarded a Nobel Prize. She shared the Nobel Prize in physics with her husband and Henri Becquerel.

Pierre Curie died suddenly in 1906. Marie Curie became the first woman to teach at the Sorbonne, a French university, when she was appointed to the professorship left vacant by the death of her husband. Continuing with her research, she found that radium could be used in the form of X-rays to reveal a picture of the interior of the body. It could also be used to destroy diseased cells.

Discovering X-Rays

The first Nobel Prize in Physics was awarded in 1901. It went to Wilhelm Conrad Roentgen of Germany. He discovered X-rays. X-rays are a form of radiation just like sunlight. However, X-rays cannot be seen. That is why nobody before Roentgen knew about them. The invisible X-rays can pass through some objects but not others. Sometimes they leave behind proof of their presence. That is how Wilhelm Roentgen discovered them.

After a radiation experiment one day, Roentgen noticed something strange. Camera film in his desk drawer had somehow been exposed. Even stranger, the exposed film bore the image of a key. Roentgen guessed that mysterious rays from his experiment were to blame. A metal key had been sitting on top of his desk. Apparently, the rays had passed through the wooden desk and exposed his film. However, the rays had not passed through the metal key. As a result, they left a shadow of the key on the film. Roentgen called his discovery X-rays. He began doing experiments to learn how they worked. Today, X-rays have many uses, especially in health care. Doctors use them to look for broken bones inside patients. Dentists use them to find tiny cavities in teeth.

Ivan Pavlov's work in classical conditioning is still studied today.

In 1934, Marie Curie died of leukemia caused by her long exposure to radiation. Sadly, in all the years she had studied uranium and radium, she never connected her own illnesses, nor those of her late husband and her assistants, with the radioactive properties of those substances. After Marie Curie's death, the Radium Institute was renamed the Curie Institute. Her notebooks, in which she recorded all her findings, are still locked up to this day—they are too radioactive to handle.

Pavlov's Dogs

In 1904, Ivan Pavlov, a scientist in St. Petersburg, Russia, won the Nobel Prize in physiology for his studies of digestion. He had been experimenting with dogs and noticed the way they would salivate or drool when they saw food. He said that this was a natural reflex because dogs needed saliva to help digest food. Pavlov began ringing a bell whenever he brought food to the dogs. They drooled when they saw the food. Then Pavlov rang the bell without bringing food. He saw that the dogs drooled anyway. Pavlov realized that they drooled because they associated the bell with the food. He called this response a conditioned reflex.

Spread of Infectious Disease

Mary Mallon, an immigrant from Ireland, was a prisoner in New York City, but she was no ordinary prisoner. She had committed no crime, and she was not locked up in jail. For three years, from 1907 to 1910, Mallon was held in Riverside Hospital in the Bronx, New York. She was considered a threat to public health.

Earlier in the decade, Mallon had caught typhoid fever. When she recovered, she went back to her job as a cook for wealthy families on Long Island. Family members in seven of the eight families for whom

Important Discoveries

The first vacuum tube was invented in 1904 by John Ambrose Fleming (1849–1945), a British electrical engineer. The vacuum tube would become an important part of radios and other electronic equipment during the first decade of the 1900s. Vacuum tubes would later be used in televisions, radar systems, telephone networks, and early computers.

In 1907, a Belgian chemist named Leo Baekeland (1863–1944) developed the first man-made plastic, or synthetic resin. This hard substance, called Bakelite, could be molded into any shape. It would also maintain its shape after being heated. Bakelite was originally used to make parts for the electrical industry. Today, it is far-fetched to imagine a world without plastics.

she had worked were struck with typhoid fever. Apparently, people who had already recovered from the disease were capable of infecting others even though they were no longer sick. Mallon was one such person. George Soper, a health worker, managed to trace the spread of the disease back to her. The bacteria, salmonella typhi, was passed from one person to another by those who had caught typhoid fever. Handling food was an easy way to transmit the bacteria to other people. Mallon was directly responsible for fifty-three cases, including three deaths, and up to another fourteen hundred cases in Ithaca, New York, in 1903. After disappearing for several years following her

Albert Einstein's theory of relativity was discounted at first.

release in 1910, Mallon was located in 1914 and imprisoned in the hospital again. This time, she was held until the day she died in 1938.

Einstein's Advances in Physics

Albert Einstein was a physicist. He sought to understand the forces of nature and the universe, and he made amazing discoveries. As a child, Albert Einstein had little interest in schoolwork. He thought his teachers were boring, and so he preferred to teach himself. At age twelve, he learned geometry on his own. The study of lines, angles, and shapes fascinated him and led him to a related field called physics. Physics is the science of matter and energy. Physicists explore natural properties, such as gravity and light.

Young Einstein had interests other than studying, such as playing the violin. Still, his favorite activity was thinking about physics. After graduating from school, he took an office job. The work was dull, but it was so easy that it gave him plenty of free time to think about how the universe works. Einstein never believed something just because it was written in a book; he always wanted proof. That trait helped him find answers to questions that other scientists had never even thought to ask.

In 1905, Einstein wrote three brilliant physics papers. They were about the nature of light and the motion of molecules. Molecules are tiny particles. Most of Einstein's peers could not grasp his amazing theories. Therefore, they chose to ignore the theories. It would take years for Albert Einstein to gain full acceptance.

Conclusion

The 1900s marked the beginning of a new era that was destined to be considered by many the American century. When the twentieth century began, there were about 1.6 billion people living in the world. When it ended, the world's population was more than 6 billion people. The enormous flow of immigrants to the United States was quickly changing the face of the nation from a predominantly rural country to one with booming cities.

The first decade of the new century was exciting. The Industrial Revolution had changed the world. It began in Britain many years earlier when people started using machines to make things. People also began working together in factories. These new methods spread around the globe. Machines and factories were soon everywhere. They gave rise to new inventions. Gains in science and medicine followed. On average, people began living longer.

In 1901, President Theodore Roosevelt ushered in two decades of progressive politics. Known as a trustbuster, Roosevelt was determined to have the government regulate corporate behavior, at least in instances where excessive greed on the part of powerful industrialists threatened public welfare. Roosevelt also became the first president to end a major strike by mediating a labor dispute. Roosevelt's administration was not always kindhearted, however. Roosevelt used the threat of military force to achieve his goals in Latin America and in other parts of the world. Other nations were given notice that, in the twentieth century, the United States would be a major player on the world stage.

Factories that produced goods would soon manufacture weapons.

This decade also marked a time of discovery and progress around the world. Scientists, such as Albert Einstein and Wilhelm Roentgen, advanced humanity's understanding of the universe. Inventors, such as Guglielmo Marconi and the Wright brothers, laid the foundations for radio communication and air travel. Thomas Edison helped bring wondrous new gadgets, including the phonograph and the electric light, into people's homes. Henry Ford made the automobile affordable. People's lives had become more comfortable. Many people looked forward to the coming years with great anticipation. It seemed that life would just keep getting better and better.

This optimism would be shattered during the next decade. Mass-production methods would be used to churn out weapons rather than automobiles or other goods to make life better. Millions of people would die in the biggest war the world had ever known. Millions more would die in a worldwide disease epidemic that science proved powerless to halt. In the United States, these tragedies would hit hard. But the country continued to expand during the decade 1910 to 1919. Two more states would be added to the Union. And America's importance on the world stage would continue to grow. Truly, it was an amazing decade.

Timeline

1900 A wave of immigration continues, during which some 9 million people will move to the United States before 1910. The minor league Western Association becomes the major league American League. William McKinley is elected president in November with Theodore Roosevelt as his vice president. First flight of a zeppelin takes place in Germany. The Boxer Rebellion erupts in China.

1901 On January 22, Great Britain's Queen Victoria dies. Pan-American Exposition takes place in Buffalo, New York, where President William McKinley is assassinated on September 6. Vice President Theodore Roosevelt becomes President. Roosevelt invites African-American leader Booker T. Washington to the White House. China's Boxer Rebellion ends. Pablo Picasso begins his Blue Period.

1902   Roosevelt becomes the first president to mediate a labor dispute. The teddy bear is introduced after President Roosevelt goes on a failed hunting trip in Mississippi in November. "In the Good Old Summertime" is released. The Roosevelt administration begins trustbusting by bringing a suit to dissolve the Northern Securities Company. By announcing that the United States Navy is ready to act, Roosevelt persuades Germany, Great Britain, and Italy to negotiate with Venezuela over a debt crisis. The United States grants Cuba independence.

1903   Edwin Porter produces *The Great Train Robbery*, the first Western movie. The Joint Playing Rules of baseball are introduced. The first World Series takes place at the end of the baseball season, in which the American League Boston Pilgrims beat the National League Pittsburgh Pirates. Congress creates the Department of Commerce and Labor. The United States urges Panamanian revolution in Colombia in order to win rights to a canal zone. In December, the Wright brothers make the world's first heavier-than-air powered flight in an airplane. Marie Curie becomes the first woman to win a Nobel Prize. Jack London's *The Call of the Wild* is published.

1904 In February, the Russo-Japanese War begins. Roosevelt runs for another term and promises Americans a Square Deal. Picasso enters his Rose Period. The world's largest subway system is completed in New York City. The World's Fair takes place in St. Louis, Missouri. Grace Weiderseim designs Campbell's Kids for soup cans. Jack London's *The Sea-Wolf* is published. "Meet Me in St. Louis" and "Give My Regards to Broadway" are released. The US Supreme Court dissolves the Northern Securities Company.

1905 On January 22, a revolution begins in Russia that results in the creation of the Duma. Roosevelt becomes the first president to travel in a submarine. Roosevelt also becomes the first president to win the Nobel Peace Prize for his role in ending the Russo-Japanese War. Albert Einstein publishes three landmark physics papers. The World's Fair is held in Portland, Oregon. A storefront theater becomes the first nickelodeon. President Roosevelt calls a football summit to decrease the dangerous violence of the sport. The second World Series is held, in which the New York Giants defeat the Philadelphia Athletics.

1906 On April 18, the San Francisco earthquake occurs, kills hundreds, and destroys huge amounts of property. Roosevelt travels to Panama to oversee work on the canal. The San

Francisco school board votes to segregate Japanese students in October. Upton Sinclair's *The Jungle* is published. Jack London's *White Fang* is published. "I'm a Yankee Doodle Dandy" is released. The United States puts down a Cuban rebellion. Congress passes the Meat Inspection Act and the Pure Food and Drug Act.

1907 Roosevelt's Gentlemen's Agreement settles a dispute over Japanese immigration to America. The electric vacuum cleaner is patented. Roosevelt sends the Great White Fleet on a tour around the world to show other nations American naval power. Mary Mallon, also known as Typhoid Mary, is taken prisoner to protect the public health. Oklahoma becomes the forty-sixth state of the Union.

1908 Henry Ford introduces the mass-produced Model T. "Take Me Out to the Ball Game" and "Shine On Harvest Moon" are released. William Howard Taft is elected president.

1909 The World's Fair is held in Seattle, Washington. "By the Light of the Silvery Moon" is released. "Maple Leaf Rag" is the most popular piano rag tune. On April 6, Robert Peary reaches the North Pole.

Glossary

assassinate—To murder an important person, such as a political figure.

blues—Music developed by rural Southern African Americans to express melancholy and woes.

cubism—An art movement that uses geometric shapes and unnatural, skewed perspective.

delegate—An agent or representative at a conference.

gentleman's agreement—Arrangement based on the trust of both or all parties rather than being legally binding.

Industrial Revolution—A period spanning the mid-eighteenth and mid-nineteenth centuries characterized by the transition to new manufacturing processes that transformed the world socially and economically.

mass production—A method of manufacturing large quantities of goods at a low cost through the use of assembly lines, machine tools, and other processes.

muckraker—A person who writes about hidden social problems.

nickelodeon—Movie theaters that cost one nickel for admission.

physicist—A scientist who studies matter and energy.

progressive—Favoring radical liberal political views.

racism—Prejudice against another race.

radiation—Energy that travels in rays or waves, such as light or X-rays.

radical—Unusual and extreme.

ragtime—Syncopated piano music developed by African-American musicians.

sanitary—Clean and free of germs.

segregation—The separation of different races or groups that is enforceable by law.

syncopated—Main trait of ragtime music in which the beats are switched so that the strong beat is weak and the weak beat is strong.

trust—A combination of businesses that are joined in order to reduce or eliminate competition and achieve complete control of the market.

Tsar—Title given to Russia's emperors before the revolution.

union—Organized association of workers formed to protect and further their rights and interests.

Further Reading

Books

Goodwin, Doris Kearns. *The Bully Pulpit: Theodore Roosevelt, William Howard Taft, and the Golden Age of Journalism.* New York.: Simon & Schuster, 2013.

Greene, Julie. *The Canal Builders: Making America's Empire at the Panama Canal.* New York: Penguin Books, 2010.

McCullough, David. *The Path Between the Seas: The Creation of the Panama Canal.* New York: Simon & Schuster, 1978.

McCullough, David. *The Wright Brothers.* New York: Simon & Schuster, 2015.

McNeese, Tim. *The Gilded Age and Progressivism.* New York: Chelsea House, 2010.

Sinclair, Upton. *The Jungle* (Dover Thrift Editions). New York: Dover Publications, 2001.

Wallenfeldt, Jeff. *U.S. Imperialism and Progressivism.* New York: Rosen Education Service, 2012.

Web Sites

thehenryford.org/exhibits/hf/default.asp

Biography of Henry Ford.

pbs.org/wgbh/amex/1900/index.html

Immersive experience about the decade.

pbs.org/wgbh/amex/wright/index.html

Explores the inventions of the Wright Brothers.

whitehouse.gov/history/presidents/tr26.html

Fact sheet about President Theodore Roosevelt.

Movies

Ragtime. Directed by Milos Forman. Hollywood, Calif.: Paramount Pictures, 1981.

Motion picture adaptation of E.L. Doctorow's historical novel.

The Roosevelts: An Intimate History. Directed by Ken Burns. Walpole, N.H.: Florentine Films, 2014.

This documentary film examines the life of Theodore Roosevelt, as well as Franklin and Eleanor Roosevelt.

Index

A

African Americans, 8, 12, 15, 35, 38, 39, 55, 68, 73
airplane, 71, 73
American Federation of Musicians, 38
American Indians, 12, 67, 68
American League (AL), 46, 49
amusement parks, 19
automobile, 7, 14, 16, 19, 44, 83

B

Baekeland, Leo, 78
baseball, 46, 47, 49
Becquerel, Henri, 74
Boston Pilgrims, 46
Boxer Rebellion, 51, 53

C

Campbell's Company, 20
Carnation, 20
Caruso, Enrico, 38
China, 11, 51, 53, 67
Civil War, 7, 35, 39, 68
Colombia, 58, 61
Coney Island, 19
Cuba, 55
Curie, Marie, 74, 77
Curie, Pierre, 74, 77

Czolgosz, Leon, 51, 54

D

Department of Commerce and Labor, 57
Du Bois, W. E. B., 15, 68

E

Einstein, Albert, 71, 80, 83
Eltinge, Julian, 35

F

fashion, 24–26
films, 35
Fleming, John Ambrose, 78
football, 43, 45
Ford, Henry, 14, 19, 83
Ford Motor Company, 19
Foy, Eddie, 35

G

General Motors, 19
Gentlemen's Agreement, 12
Gibson, Charles Dana, 24
Gibson Girls, 35
"Give My Regards to Broadway", 38
Gould, Jay, 53

Great Britain, 7, 51, 65, 81
Great Train Robbery, The, 35
Great White Fleet, 67

H

Handy, W. C. ("Father of the Blues"), 40
Henson, Matthew, 73

I

immigration, 9, 11, 12, 16, 81
Intercollegiate Athletic Association (IAA), 45
Intercollegiate Rules Committee, 45
"In the Good Old Summertime," 38

J

Japan, 11, 12, 51, 62, 63, 65, 67
Jim Crow laws, 12
Johnson, Byron Bancroft "Ban", 46
"Joint Playing Rules", 46
Jolson, Al, 35
Joplin, Scott, 38
Jungle, The, 29

K

Keller, Helen, 30
Knabenshue, Roy, 73

L

Langley, Samuel, 73
London, Jack, 11

lynching, 15

M

Mallon, Mary, 77, 78, 80
Manly, Charles, 73
"Maple Leaf Rag", 38
Marconi, Guglielmo, 10, 83
mass production, 14, 19, 24, 83
McGraw, John, 46
McKinley, William, 51, 54, 55, 57
Meat Inspection Act, 30
"Meet Me in St. Louis", 38
Mitchell, John, 58
Mitchom, Morris, 22
Mitchom, Rose, 22
Morgan, John Pierpont (J. P.), 57
muckrakers, 29

N

National Association for the Advancement of Colored People (NAACP), 15, 68
National League (NL), 46
New York City, 16, 19, 27, 36, 46, 53, 68, 73, 77
New York Giants, 46, 49
Nicholas II, Tsar of Russia, 65
nickelodeon, 35, 36
Northern Securities Company, 57, 63
North Pole, 71, 73, 74

O

October Manifesto, 65
Olympic Games, 49, 50

P

Panama Canal, 58, 60, 61, 63
Pan-American Exposition, 51, 54
Pavlov, Ivan, 77
Peary, Robert Edwin, 73, 74
Philadelphia Athletics, 49
Philippines, 55, 67
phonograph, 29, 34, 38, 83
Picasso, Pablo, 40
Pittsburgh Pirates, 46
Porter, Edwin, 32
Progressive Era, 53
Pure Food and Drug Act, 30

R

racism, 8, 12, 15, 68
ragtime, 29, 38, 40
Rainey, Ma ("Mother of the
  Blues"), 39
Roentgen, Wilhelm, 75, 83
Roosevelt, Theodore, 7, 8, 12, 21,
  22, 24, 29, 30, 43, 51, 53, 55, 57,
  58, 63, 65, 67, 81
Russia, 62, 63, 65, 77
Russo-Japanese War, 62, 63, 65

S

San Francisco, California, 11
San Francisco earthquake (1906),
  11
Saturday Evening Post, 20
sheet music, 38
Sherman Antitrust Act, 55, 57
Sinclair, Upton, 29, 30, 31
slavery, 12, 39, 68

Soper, George, 78
Spain, 40, 55, 67
Spanish-American War, 55, 67
Square Deal, 63
Steeplechase Park, 19
streetcars, 16, 19
subway, 16
Sullivan, Anne, 30

T

teddy bear, 22, 24
Tewksbury, J.W.B., 50
Tin Pan Alley, 38
trustbusting, 57, 81
Tucker, Sophie, 35
Tuskegee Institute, 15
Typhoid Mary. *See* Mallon, Mary.

U

United Mine Workers (UMW),
  58
United States Congress, 57, 67,
  74
United States Navy, 7, 55, 61, 65
United States Supreme Court, 57
uranium, 74, 77

V

vaudeville, 29, 35
Victoria, Queen of England, 24

W

Washington, Booker T., 15
Western Association (WA), 46
Western movies, 35

Williams, Bert, 35
World Series, 46, 47, 49
World's Fair, 20, 50
Wright brothers, 63, 71, 72, 73,
  83
Wynn, Ed, 35

X

X-rays, 71, 74, 75

Y

Young, Cy, 47

Z

zeppelin, 73